MW01234334

WHAT LIBERALS HAVE DONE FOR AMERICA

AND WHY THEY DESERVE RESPECT

HERBERT WASHINGTON PHD

WHAT LIBERALS HAVE DONE FOR AMERICA

WHAT LIBERALS HAVE DONE FOR AMERICA

.

WHAT LIBERALS HAVE DONE FOR AMERICA

WHAT LIBERALS HAVE DONE FOR AMERICA

WHAT LIBERALS HAVE DONE FOR AMERICA

WHAT LIBERALS HAVE DONE FOR AMERICA

WHAT LIBERALS HAVE DONE FOR AMERICA

WHAT LIBERALS HAVE DONE FOR AMERICA

WHAT LIBERALS HAVE DONE FOR AMERICA

WHAT LIBERALS HAVE DONE FOR AMERICA

WHAT LIBERALS HAVE DONE FOR AMERICA

WHAT LIBERALS HAVE DONE FOR AMERICA

WHAT LIBERALS HAVE DONE FOR AMERICA

WHAT LIBERALS HAVE DONE FOR AMERICA

WHAT LIBERALS HAVE DONE FOR AMERICA

WHAT LIBERALS HAVE DONE FOR AMERICA

WHAT LIBERALS HAVE DONE FOR AMERICA

WHAT LIBERALS HAVE DONE FOR AMERICA

WHAT LIBERALS HAVE DONE FOR AMERICA

WHAT LIBERALS HAVE DONE FOR AMERICA

WHAT LIBERALS HAVE DONE FOR AMERICA

WHAT LIBERALS HAVE DONE FOR AMERICA

WHAT LIBERALS HAVE DONE FOR AMERICA

WHAT LIBERALS HAVE DONE FOR AMERICA

WHAT LIBERALS HAVE DONE FOR AMERICA

WHAT LIBERALS HAVE DONE FOR AMERICA

.

WHAT LIBERALS HAVE DONE FOR AMERICA

WHAT LIBERALS HAVE DONE FOR AMERICA

WHAT LIBERALS HAVE DONE FOR AMERICA

WHAT LIBERALS HAVE DONE FOR AMERICA

WHAT LIBERALS HAVE DONE FOR AMERICA

WHAT LIBERALS HAVE DONE FOR AMERICA

WHAT LIBERALS HAVE DONE FOR AMERICA

WHAT LIBERALS HAVE DONE FOR AMERICA

WHAT LIBERALS HAVE DONE FOR AMERICA

WHAT LIBERALS HAVE DONE FOR AMERICA

WHAT LIBERALS HAVE DONE FOR AMERICA

WHAT LIBERALS HAVE DONE FOR AMERICA

WHAT LIBERALS HAVE DONE FOR AMERICA

WHAT LIBERALS HAVE DONE FOR AMERICA

WHAT LIBERALS HAVE DONE FOR AMERICA

WHAT LIBERALS HAVE DONE FOR AMERICA

WHAT LIBERALS HAVE DONE FOR AMERICA

WHAT LIBERALS HAVE DONE FOR AMERICA

WHAT LIBERALS HAVE DONE FOR AMERICA

WHAT LIBERALS HAVE DONE FOR AMERICA

WHAT LIBERALS HAVE DONE FOR AMERICA

WHAT LIBERALS HAVE DONE FOR AMERICA

WHAT LIBERALS HAVE DONE FOR AMERICA

WHAT LIBERALS HAVE DONE FOR AMERICA

WHAT LIBERALS HAVE DONE FOR AMERICA

WHAT LIBERALS HAVE DONE FOR AMERICA

WHAT LIBERALS HAVE DONE FOR AMERICA

WHAT LIBERALS HAVE DONE FOR AMERICA

WHAT LIBERALS HAVE DONE FOR AMERICA

WHAT LIBERALS HAVE DONE FOR AMERICA

WHAT LIBERALS HAVE DONE FOR AMERICA

WHAT LIBERALS HAVE DONE FOR AMERICA

WHAT LIBERALS HAVE DONE FOR AMERICA

WHAT LIBERALS HAVE DONE FOR AMERICA

WHAT LIBERALS HAVE DONE FOR AMERICA

WHAT LIBERALS HAVE DONE FOR AMERICA

WHAT LIBERALS HAVE DONE FOR AMERICA

WHAT LIBERALS HAVE DONE FOR AMERICA

WHAT LIBERALS HAVE DONE FOR AMERICA

WHAT LIBERALS HAVE DONE FOR AMERICA

Made in the USA
Las Vegas, NV
18 May 2025

22341745R00056